CONTEMPORARY LIVES

PINK

POP SINGER & SONGWRITER

ABDO
Publishing Company

CONTEMPORARY LIVES

PINK

POP SINGER & SONGWRITER

by Rebecca Rowell

CREDITS

Published by ABDO Publishing Company, PO Box 398166, Minneapolis, MN 55439. Copyright © 2014 by Abdo Consulting Group, Inc. International copyrights reserved in all countries. No part of this book may be reproduced in any form without written permission from the publisher. The Essential Library™ is a trademark and logo of ABDO Publishing Company.

Printed in the United States of America,
North Mankato, Minnesota
092013
012014

 THIS BOOK CONTAINS AT LEAST 10% RECYCLED MATERIALS.

Editor: Angela Wiechmann
Series Designer: Emily Love

Photo credits: Shutterstock Images, cover, 3, 15, 55, 69, 70, 74, 79, 97 (bottom), 100; Matt Sayles/AP Images, 6, 9, 12, 66, 99 (top); Seth Poppel/ Yearbook Library, 16, 20, 25; Jim Cooper/AP Images, 26, 97 (top); Helga Esteb/Shutterstock Images, 29, 38; Kristi Miller/Newspix/Rex USA, 33; Fox/ Photofest, 34; Delly Carr/AP Images, 40; Featureflash/Shutterstock Images, 42, 96; Jim Cooper/AP Images, 44, 51; John D McHugh/AP Images, 49; Keystone/Laurent Gillieron/AP Images, 52; Jeff Christensen/AP Images, 59; Keystone/Peter Klaunzer/AP Images, 60; AP Images, 63, 88; Kevin Winter/ Getty Images, 80, 98; Martin Karius/Rex USA, 85; Rex Features/AP Images, 87, 99 (bottom); Charles Sykes/Invision/AP Images, 91; Matt Sayles/Invision/ AP Images, 95

Library of Congress Control Number: 2013913364

Cataloging-in-Publication Data

Rowell, Rebecca.
 Pink: pop singer & songwriter / Rebecca Rowell.
   p. cm. -- (Contemporary lives)
Includes bibliographical references and index.
ISBN 978-1-62403-226-4
1. Pink, 1979- --Juvenile literature. 2. Singers--United States--Biography-- Juvenile literature.   1. Title.
782.42164092--dc23
[B]

2013913364

CONTENTS

Pink's performance at the 2010 Grammys was a spectacular display.

CHAPTER 1

"Glitter in the Air"

||||||||||||||||||||||||||||||||||||||||||||||

The auditorium darkened at the 2010 Grammy Awards ceremony. The camera showed a stage filled with screens awash in red. The image quickly changed to shades of blue moving in a pattern reminiscent of water. A piano began playing the first notes of the song "Glitter in the Air." Notes from a guitar punctuated the piano's melody. The camera zoomed in closer and closer to a figure walking between the screens. The figure's voice rang out before the spotlight revealed she was the pop star Pink. Her voice was a little shaky at first—nerves that lasted only a few notes.

The 30-year-old was dressed in white. A cover-up hung loosely over her body, its hood around her head and its fabric trailing behind her. Pink walked as she sang, making her way to the front of the stage, then down steps, proceeding until she reached the theater floor. She stood in an aisle between rows and rows of seats. Her music-industry colleagues were seated on both sides of her.

The powerful singer with an undeniable independent streak finished the second verse in the aisle. There, she removed the cover-up, pulling the large neckline open and past her shoulders, then letting it drop to the floor. Underneath, Pink

JUMP IN SALES

Grammy performances often boost music sales. This was definitely the case for Pink after her 2010 Grammy performance. "Glitter in the Air" is featured on the star's *Funhouse* album. *Funhouse* sales increased a whopping 234 percent the week following her appearance on the live awards show.[1]

Pink appeared in a cover-up before shedding it to reveal a bodysuit adorned with fabric strips and sparkles.

was dressed in a revealing flesh-toned bodysuit accented with white, asymmetrical strips of fabric and silver glittery sequins. She continued ahead to a smaller round stage in the middle of the auditorium, walking tall in matching silver glitter high heels.

Pink ascended the steps to the stage, an island in the midst of the crowd. Four women were there. They were gold from head to toe: hair, skin, and bikinis. Three of the women were lifted into the air, dangling from blue silk slung under each dancer's

Pink's performance of "Glitter in the Air" at the Grammys was not a new act. She had been performing the song as a Cirque du Soleil–style act during her 2009 tour promoting *Funhouse*, her fifth album. Michael Menachem of *Billboard* magazine wrote of her performance at New York's famed Madison Square Garden: "When Pink finally touched down, she continued singing with bombast, as though the entire spectacle had been no sweat. If the rest of the show hadn't already made the case that Pink has one of the best pop-rock voices—and the most brazen moves—of her generation of stars, this final moment certainly did."[2]

arms and behind her back. The apparatus holding the fabric rotated the women around in a circle, like a ride at an amusement park.

The fourth gold woman was crouched down. She helped Pink into her own silks, holding open the white fabric to cradle the singer, similar to the way a hammock surrounds a person when he or she sits. In the center of the circle formed by the dancers, Pink rose with the silks. She leaned back, and the fourth woman gave her a gentle push to make her spin. The equipment lifted Pink and her dancers higher and higher into the air. The dancers moved their arms and legs in rhythm as Pink sang: "There you are, sitting in the garden, clutching my coffee. Calling me sugar."[3]

With her head tilted back, Pink was essentially singing upside down. As music played between verses, the apparatus lowered the singer. She disappeared from view, lowered inside an opening in the small stage. She then reappeared dripping wet. She was still in the silks, stretched out horizontally, ankles crossed, rotating, with water flying.

She shifted her position as she sang, moving the fabric so it was under her arms and behind her back. She was right-side up. Next she changed position again, hooking one leg around the silk so she could dangle upside down. She sang, "Have you ever held your breath and asked yourself will

AFRAID OF FALLING

After the 2010 Grammys, Pink admitted she had been afraid of falling during the dizzying performance. She explained, "When I do it on tour, I don't have lights above me. There were lights above me [at the Grammys], so it almost went into a strobe thing, and I actually did get a little turned around. I thought . . . I was going to fall. . . . But I worked it out."[4]

Pink capped her performance with a heart-stopping upside-down spin.

it ever get better than tonight?"[5] She then wrapped her other leg around the silk, making her body completely vertical and upside down. Pulling in her arms, she spun faster and faster, water whipping from her.

All the while, the equipment overhead carried Pink and her singers through the air, above the audience, and back to the main stage. The machinery seemed invisible as eyes focused on the singer. The apparatus lowered her to the stage as she repositioned with the silks under her arms and behind her back. As the music slowed, so did Pink's spinning. The crowd cheered.

Pink landed on the stage. The acrobatic singer held on to the silks to steady herself after such a dizzying spin. Then she took a bow. As the lights came up in the auditorium, the camera panned the audience. They were standing in ovation and clapping in awe.

||||||||||||||||||||||||||||||||||||||||||||||||||||||||||

SEASONED PERFORMER

"Glitter in the Air" is not typical Pink fare. Hitting the scene in 2000 with her first album, *Can't Take*

Me Home, Pink is known for fast-tempo songs such as "Get the Party Started" and "U + Ur Hand." "Glitter in the Air" is a quiet, piano-heavy ballad about love. Pink cowrote the tune, revealing she is much more than the tough party girl her reputation often brings to mind.

The Pennsylvania native is much more than a rocker. She is as real as anyone. She has a range of emotions. She has ups and downs. But she is seemingly unafraid of any question—or any person.

The road to Pink's standout performance at the Grammys on January 31, 2010, had been a long one. Her journey was marked with personal and

"She's a career artist, unafraid to take risks and deal with the repercussions, and as such, she'll still be here long after her contemporaries have disappeared. Then again, if she keeps dangling upside down, she might not make it that long. And, really, she shouldn't have to go to such lengths (or heights) to be loved. Though, now that I think of it, she wouldn't be Pink if she didn't."[6]

—JAMES MONTGOMERY, MTV.COM

In the air and on the red carpet, Pink made a strong statement at the 2010 Grammys.

professional challenges, beginning with a rocky family life when she was a child. But achievements were ahead, too, for her career and her life.

Through it all, Pink remained true to herself. She is a strong woman with an undeniable voice of independence and strength. She has a distinct style—in music and in fashion—that can be identified with a simple word, her name: Pink.

||||||||||

Before she became Pink, Alecia Beth Moore, *front center*, was a young teen with a rocky life.

CHAPTER 2
Pink's Roots

||||||||||||||||||||||||||||||||||||||||||||||||||||||||||||||||||||||||||||

Pink was born Alecia Beth Moore on September 8, 1979, in Doylestown, Pennsylvania. She is the younger of James and Judy Moore's two children. Brother Jason was two when Alecia arrived.

Alecia and her brother grew up in a middle-class family. Her father was a veteran of the Vietnam War (1954–1975). He worked in the insurance industry. Her mother worked as a nurse.

||||||||||||||||||||||||||||||||||||||

A SHAKY START

Alecia's parents had a troubled relationship. Eventually, the couple split. In 1987, when Alecia was eight years old, her parents divorced. Alecia was particularly close to her father. James was musical and played guitar. He shared his love of music with young Alecia. She listened to a variety of records from her father's collection, including Patsy Cline, Billy Joel, and Joni Mitchell.

> "I knew at two or three that I'd be a singer. I believe that you sign up for this life before you get here. . . . I never pictured anything else."[2]
>
> —PINK, SEPTEMBER 18, 2012

Alecia showed an affinity for music from the time she was very little. She was always humming or singing. Sometimes, her dad would ask her to pick a new song because he was tired of hearing her sing the same one over and over. She responded matter-of-factly, "Dad, I'm practicing. I'm going to be a star someday. And I have to be good at it."[1]

Alecia began taking voice lessons when she was nine years old. Music helped her cope with her parents' struggles. She described what life at home felt like to her as a youth:

> When it's World War III in your house every day, that's not a fun place to be. Singing was the only thing I knew I was good at, the only way I could get people to listen to me, the only way I could get my mom and dad in the same room. I'd sing what I had to say.[3]

Her parents' split contributed to young Alecia's rebellious side. She began smoking and skateboarding. She also spent time with kids who used drugs and were considered punks. Adults were wary of her—even her own parents. As she noted,

> I was never allowed to go over to any of my friends' houses when I was little, because I was a bad influence. None of their parents liked me and my own parents were scared to death of me—and for me.[4]

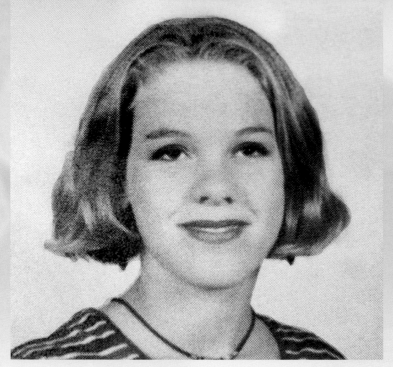

A troubled teen, Alecia found herself in risky places making risky decisions.

DANGEROUS CHOICES

Alecia began focusing on music. It was an outlet for her feelings. When she was 12, she established her first band with others who enjoyed music. She also got her first tattoo.

She began exploring music in places she really was not supposed to be. Doylestown, Alecia's hometown, is a small city in the southeast part of the state, 39 miles (63 km) north of Philadelphia. She started going to clubs in Philadelphia when she was 13 years old. She got in using a fake ID.

In the clubs, she quickly gained valuable experience singing and dancing. Alecia first performed in Philadelphia nightclubs as a dancer. She then moved on to singing backup for Schoolz of Thought, a local hip-hop group. At age 14, she began writing songs. These activities were not simply passing fads. Alecia was becoming a versatile performer.

Alecia may have been having fun and enjoying music, but she was also taking risks. The young teen was not coming home by curfew and would sometimes disappear for lengths of time. She partied heavily. She smoked, drank alcohol, and used and sold drugs.

Partying, alcohol, and drugs were not Alecia's best choices. She was rebellious in other ways, too. Alecia was arrested for petty theft and trespassing.

TIMELINE OF ADDICTION ||||||||||||||||||||||||||||||||||||||||||||||||||

In a 2012 interview with VH1, Pink shared a timeline of her substance abuse as a child: She started smoking cigarettes when she was nine years old. She added marijuana when she was

11. By the time she was 13, Alecia was doing PCP, Ecstasy, and crystal meth. She gave up drugs forever after almost overdosing at age 15.

At 15, she dropped out of high school. Alecia has stated of her behavior, "I was uncontrollable. I was just awful."[5] Not knowing what else to do with her daughter, Alecia's mom kicked the teen out. It was not an easy decision, and she regretted it. Alecia moved in with her father, James, who lived nearby. The move did not stop her clubbing. She continued spending considerable time at nightclubs. Alecia's father also was concerned for his daughter: "I was frightened to death for her. I did a lot of praying."[6]

TURNING POINT

November 1995 was a turning point for Alecia. On Thanksgiving, 15-year-old Alecia took a combination of drugs, including PCP, cocaine, crystal meth, and marijuana. She almost overdosed, and she passed out. But Alecia was scheduled to sing that night at a club, so a friend roused her. Alecia got to Club Fever and sang. The disc jockey recognized her talent and offered the teen the opportunity to sing on the main stage the following night as well—an even bigger opportunity. He had

Because she dropped out of high school when she was 15 years old, Alecia did not receive a high school diploma. However, she does have a general equivalency diploma, or GED. She accomplished this milestone in 1998. To qualify for a GED, a person has to pass tests on a variety of subjects, including reading, writing, math, science, and social studies.

one condition: no drugs. She wanted to perform, so she stopped taking them.

Alecia was eager to sing. But the nearly all-black audience was angry as she took the stage. People wondered who this white girl thought she was, singing music by Mary J. Blige, a popular black rhythm and blues (R&B) singer. But Alecia refused to be intimidated, and she won over the crowd. She was determined to become a musician. "There was never a point where I didn't think I would do this," she explained of that time. "There was never a point in my life where I even thought something else was an option."[7]

During this time, she got a new name: Pink. She often styles it as P!nk, with an exclamation point instead of the letter i. The name has multiple sources. One origin is that a friend named Alecia after Mr. Pink, a character in the movie *Reservoir Dogs*. Another possibility is that the nickname comes from the fact that young Alecia blushed easily and turned pink. Finally, because Alecia was a white girl in clubs frequented predominantly by African Americans, the nickname described her skin color.

Alecia's family life was heartbreaking, and her behavior was risky. But Alecia survived, and these experiences shaped the artist she would become. In a 2006 interview, the singer explained, "I've never fitted in. I just wanted to get . . . out of that town and get on with my life."[8] Her talent would allow her to do just that, but she would have to be discovered first.

||||||||||

"I was a dark teenager. When I was 17 or 18, I had not yet exorcised my demons. My anger is more focused now. Maybe I'm less certain and more open to negotiation. I used to be angry with everyone. I got a lot of that from my dad. He was tough, and I was raised with that fighter attitude."[9]

—PINK, SEPTEMBER 18, 2012

Alecia's roller coaster experiences as a teenager would motivate her toward success.

A talented teen, Alecia would be handpicked to join R&B groups and eventually launch a solo career.

CHAPTER 3
Getting Signed

||||||||||||||||||||||||||||||||||||||||||||||||||||||||||||||||||||||||||||

The time Alecia spent in Philadelphia nightclubs as a teenager in the early 1990s was not in vain. Dealing and doing drugs were bad choices, but they were lessons that would shape her life personally and professionally. And singing and dancing allowed the teenager to express herself in productive ways. Performing in nightclubs also allowed her to hone her skills. And it was where she would be discovered.

|||||||||||||||||||||||||||||||||||||

CHOICE

One night, someone with MCA record company asked the talented teen to audition to be part of the R&B group Basic Instinct. Alecia did well and became a member. The group had a recording contract and went to work in a studio. Even so, the group did not succeed and broke up after two years.

The 16-year-old moved on and became part of the all-girl trio Choice in 1995. They sang R&B and pop. The trio auditioned for record companies and finally caught the attention of Antonio "L. A." Reid, cofounder of LaFace Records. The music executive offered the group a record deal in 1996.

IN-YOUR-FACE ATTITUDE

Before signing with Reid, Choice visited various music companies to audition, hoping to make it big. On one occasion, the trio sang for Tommy Mottola, a music executive. Alecia and her groupmates had launched into their first song for the bigwig when she noticed he was not really paying attention. She promptly stopped the singing. The teen demanded Mottola's attention, saying, "Can you at least act like you're paying attention and not look out the . . . window while we're singing, because I didn't smoke today."[1]

L. A. Reid would become a mentor and guiding force for Alecia.

The three young women accepted the offer and moved to Atlanta, Georgia, to record an album.

While making the album, producer Daryl Simmons asked Alecia to write a bridge for the song "Just to Be Loving You." The teenager delivered and impressed Simmons as well as Reid.

But Choice did not last. There were differences over the direction the group should take musically. Specifically, Reid told Alecia to go solo or go home. He recognized her talent and thought she should pursue a career as a singer but not as part of a group. It was a difficult decision for the aspiring

> Reid spoke about discovering Pink. He was surprised by her talent. Reid said of Pink, "It's pretty rare to find a young, 16-year-old white girl to be singing with so much soul. She's not even old enough to be soulful yet."[3]

singer. Her groupmates were like her sisters. They even lived together. But Alecia made the choice to push forward as a solo artist. The group disbanded in 1998. Following Choice's end, Reid offered Alecia a record deal as a solo artist. And Alecia took one step closer to stardom.

During this time, the aspiring star made her nickname her stage name. From then on, she would be known by a single four-letter word, sometimes stylized with an exclamation point. P!nk had arrived. As Reid stated, "One week she's Alecia Moore, and a week later, she shows up at my office and she's Pink."[2]

||||||||||||||||||||||||||||||||||||||||||||||||||||||

CAN'T TAKE ME HOME

Pink went to work, penning songs with a collection of songwriters. She cowrote seven of the album's

13 tracks. LaFace released Pink's first album, *Can't Take Me Home*, on May 5, 2000.

The 20-year-old's debut album was a success, at least in terms of sales. Its 13 R&B and dance-pop tracks appealed to buyers. By the end of the year, the album sold 4 million copies.[4] The album spawned three Top 10 hits: "There You Go," "Most Girls," and "You Make Me Sick." In addition, "There You Go" received another honor—it was her first gold record.

Critically, it was not as successful. Douglas Wolk reviewed the album for the iconic *Rolling Stone* magazine. He gave it two and a half stars out of a possible five. He wrote of Pink's debut effort that she had a "dazzling, gymnastic R&B

"Nobody came to me and said, 'OK, we're going to call you Pink. Here, throw on some pink hair, put on some pink shirts, here you go, just be you.' No, this is me. This is who I am, my music. I don't try to be candy-coated. I don't try to walk on eggshells. I am what I am. Love me or hate me."[5]

—PINK, MARCH 1, 2011

voice" and one great single with "There You Go."[6] Otherwise, he said she was unoriginal.

In summer 2000, Pink went on tour to promote her album. She was the opening act for *NSYNC, a popular boy group. Pink toured with 98 Degrees, another all-male singing group, as well. For a joke, the mischievous Pink covered 98 Degrees' bus with toilet paper. Pink was having fun while on the road.

||||||||||||||||||||||||||||||||||||||||||||||||||||||||||||

SUCCESSFUL, BUT NOT SATISFIED

Can't Take Me Home was a sales success. Multiple singles from the debut release received considerable radio play. And Pink was busy touring with popular boy bands. By all accounts, the new artist was a success.

GOING GOLD—AND BEYOND ||||||||||||||||||||||||||||||||||||||||||||||||||||||||

The Recording Industry Association of America (RIAA) awards artists when sales reach certain marks. The RIAA certifies record and album sales of 500,000 units as gold, 1 million units as platinum, and 2 million units as multiplatinum. Several of Pink's songs and all of her albums have received one or more of these certifications.

With her first album and her career officially on its way, Pink had arrived.

But she was not satisfied. She was more than just another teen act typical of the genre at the time. Her musical interests and talents went deeper than the sound created on her first album. Pink wanted to do more musically. As she explained, "There was no blood, sweat, or tears on my first album—and no emotional exchange between me and the musicians. R&B is a conveyor belt."[7] Pink wanted a change, and she set about making that happen.

In 2001, Pink was ready to burst out with a new sound.

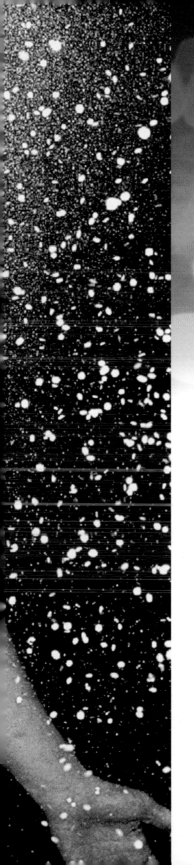

CHAPTER 4

Evolving Her Sound

IIIIIIIIIIIIIIIIIIIIIIIIIIIIIIIIIIIIIIIIIIIIIIIIIIIIIIII

n 2000, Pink's career as a solo artist got off to a good start. But the R&B and dance-pop styles on her first album were not what she wanted to perform. She wanted to do more with her music. She wanted to rock out.

IIIIIIIIIIIIIIIIIIIIIIIIIIIIIIIIIIII

"LADY MARMALADE"

The year 2001 took Pink down an edgier path musically. That year, she collaborated with Christina Aguilera, Lil' Kim, and Mýa on "Lady Marmalade." The song was a remake of the 1970s hit by the girl group Labelle. The remake was for the sound track of *Moulin Rouge!*, a movie musical.

"Lady Marmalade" reached Number 1 on the charts. Pink and the other singers won the 2001 Grammy for Best Pop Collaboration with Vocals.

FEUDING WITH AGUILERA

Pink and Aguilera collaborated on "Lady Marmalade" and shared in the accolades the work generated, but the two women are not friends. Before recording began for the popular remake, Aguilera attended a meeting with Pink and the other singers. Aguilera was escorted by Ron Fair, the music executive who discovered and signed her to a recording contract. He was also the song's producer. Without greeting anyone or introducing himself, he decided which part Aguilera would sing in the song: the high part, the part featured most. Pink was not pleased with Fair's behavior. She responded, "Hi. How are you? So nice of you to introduce yourself. I'm Pink. She will not be taking that part. I think that's what the . . . meeting is about."[1] This first exchange set the tone for a tense relationship over the years.

Pink said, "When I won the Grammy I was happy and my parents were proud, but I felt like I was winning it for the team."[2] Pink wanted to release some of her inner world. She believed doing so would help her become the songwriter and artist she aspired to become.

‖‖‖

RECORDING M!SSUNDAZTOOD

In 2001, Pink also worked on her second album. From the start, Pink wanted to take *M!ssundaztood* in an edgier, tougher direction than the R&B–styled *Can't Take Me Home*. Initially, producer Reid did not support Pink's vision. He was afraid she would lose her fan base. But Pink was firm in her stance and would not back down from pursuing her desire. After two weeks, Reid finally agreed to let Pink go in the direction she wanted.

For this album, Pink collaborated with songwriter and producer Linda Perry. Perry had been the lead singer of the 1990s rock group 4 Non Blondes. She was Pink's idol when the young aspiring star was struggling at home.

For *M!ssundaztood*, Pink collaborated with her idol, Linda Perry.

Perry had not had much success since 1992 and seemed to have disappeared from the music scene. Upon meeting, the two women had a connection from the start. Perry helped Pink achieve the tougher sound the rising star was looking for. More than that, the experienced songwriter encouraged Pink to craft songs and express her inner world. Pink cowrote 11 of the album's 14 songs. Pink felt understood for the first time.

FINDING LOVE

Pink's personal life hit new heights in 2001 as well. Pink met star motocross rider Carey Hart at the X Games in 2001. The X Games highlight the best in extreme sports, including BMX, motocross, skateboarding, snowboarding, and surfing. Right after meeting Pink, Hart took to the track. Racing up a jump, he launched high into the air. Then he crashed into the ground and broke more than a dozen bones. Seeing the crash, Pink feared Hart was dead. After such an emotional reaction, she decided she would never date a motocross racer.

She quickly went against her own words. Two weeks later, the singer and racer met again. They fell for each other and started dating. They were very happy when together, but found it challenging to make time for the relationship with such busy careers.

||||||||||||||||||||||||||||||||||||||||||||||||||||||||||

M!SSUNDAZTOOD IS A HIT

With a new relationship and a new album ready to launch, Pink was riding high. The first single hit airwaves on November 1, 2001. Written by

Pink fell in love with Carey Hart, a motocross racer who performed death-defying stunts.

Perry, "Get the Party Started" was a radio success, breaking into the Top 5. LaFace released the album that same month, on November 20. Boosted by the popularity of "Get the Party Started," the 22-year-old's second album eventually went five times platinum on October 22, 2003, selling more than 10 million copies.[3]

"Don't Let Me Get Me" was the second single from the album. Pink addressed her experiences as a teen as well as in the music industry, referencing producer L. A. Reid: "L. A. told me, 'You'll be a pop star. All you have to change is everything you are.'"[4] The song gave Pink another Top 10 hit. As for Reid, he described *M!ssundaztood* as the type of album that defines a career. He acknowledged

PINK THE ACTRESS

In 2002, as *M!ssundaztood* was climbing the charts, Pink made her movie debut. She appeared as a rock singer in the film *Rollerball*, which stars LL Cool J, Chris Klein, and Rebecca Romijn-Stamos. Pink would go on to appear in several films during her career. Some roles would be quick cameos, such as for the films *Charlie's Angels: Full Throttle* (2003) and *Get Him to the Greek* (2010). Other roles were more substantial.

In 2007, Pink would receive top billing as an actress in a movie. She starred with Shannyn Sossamon in the horror thriller *Catacombs*. Her given name, Alecia Moore, was listed just above the title on the poster. In 2011, Pink voiced the character Gloria in the animated film *Happy Feet Two*. By 2013, Pink would receive praise for her role in *Thanks for Sharing*, costarring Mark Ruffalo and Gwyneth Paltrow.

As sales rocketed for *M!ssundaztood*, Pink knew her stronger, edgier direction was a hit with fans.

Pink's wise choice in changing directions, despite his initial resistance.

Critics also noted the album's new direction. *Rolling Stone* reviewer Rob Sheffield awarded the new album three stars out of five. He wrote: "Pink deserves respect for expressing herself instead of going through the teen-pop motions—even if her execution isn't up to her ambitions."[5]

UPS AND DOWNS OF TOURING

Pink went on a tour to promote M!ssundaztood, called Pink's Party Tour 2002. She was a headliner now, no longer just an opening act for other groups.

In 2001 and 2002, Hart and Pink were doing the best they could while Pink's career skyrocketed. But with touring keeping them apart, it proved to be too much for Pink. In 2002, they broke up.

Despite the personal lows, Pink's career was at a high. She had created music truer to herself. Even better, her work was well received by critics and fans alike. Only time would tell what she had in store next.

||||||||||

With *Try This*, her third album, Pink hoped to launch into new success.

CHAPTER 5

Try This

||||||||||||||||||||||||||||||||||||||||||

By the end of 2002, 23-year-old Pink had established herself as an artist of note. With her second album and subsequent tour, the young singer proved she was a force in terms of music and personality. But she could not rest on her past success. Pink needed to keep her career moving forward.

||||||||||||||||||||||||||||||||||||

Pink helped relaunch her idol Perry's career after working together on *M!ssundaztood*. With the career boost, Perry started collaborating with other singers. Chief among them was Aguilera, for whom Perry wrote the hit "Beautiful." Pink was not pleased, as Aguilera was something of a rival to her. Pink worked much less with Perry on *Try This*. Eventually, the two had a falling out.

A NEW ALBUM

In 2003, Pink headed back into the recording studio to work on her third album, *Try This*. She cowrote all of the album's 13 tracks. Perry, who had helped craft the edgier sound on *M!ssundaztood*, worked on *Try This* as well, but to a lesser degree. She contributed to two songs. Pink worked primarily with Tim Armstrong, lead singer of the punk rock band Rancid. The pair wrote together for two weeks, composing ten songs. Eight of them ended up on the final product.

The album was released on November 11, 2003. With *Try This*, Pink advanced the edgier sound she created on *M!ssundaztood*. But she also included a track reminiscent of her initial work, the R&B–style *Can't Take Me Home*. A *Rolling Stone* reviewer noted: "With Pink's transformation nearly complete, the lone R&B slow jam 'Catch Me While I'm Sleeping,' which would have fit just fine on her debut, sounds downright out of place here."[1]

Pink's musical evolution was also evident in "Waiting for Love," the album's seventh track. While Pink had written many songs in her young life, she had not written one about love until "Waiting for Love." Pink was well aware of the milestone. She said of the tune, "This is my first love song. I've only ever written hate songs."[2]

||||||||||||||||||||||||||||||||||||||||||||||||||||||||||||

LESS SUCCESSFUL

Try This allowed Pink to continue down her path of expression and exploration. Collaborating with Armstrong, she created music with a harder sound

LIKE OLD FRIENDS ||||||||||||||||||||||||||||||||||||||||||||||||||||||||||||||||||

In an MTV interview from October 2003, Tim Armstrong described his personal relationship with

years. He said, "I was like, 'Yo, this is my homegirl. If I grew up with you, I'd roll with you. You'd be my girl.'

> "I'd rather fall down for what I believe in and for what makes me tick. Is that smart? Who knows. Might not be. But there's still some fear in me—I want to be understood, I want to be heard."[4]
>
> —PINK, NOVEMBER 8, 2003

than that of her first album. And *Try This* spawned another popular radio song as "Trouble" landed on *Billboard*'s Top 40. But it was not nearly as successful as some of her previous radio hits, such as "Get the Party Started" or "Just Like a Pill."

In terms of sales, *Try This* went platinum by December, but it did not do nearly as well as *M!ssundaztood*. However, critical reviews were perhaps better than sales would have suggested. Barry Walters of *Rolling Stone* gave her three stars out of five. He noted,

> *After* M!ssundaztood, *her choices were to repeat herself or to try more material outside her realm of expertise. She does a little of both on* Try This, *with mixed results. . . . Like it or not, Pink is stuck with the crucial punk dilemma of how to grow up and make maturity matter. Whether*

Try This received good reviews, but it failed to live up to the whopping success of M!ssundaztood.

she'll squander her rage or rise to the challenge remains to be seen.[5]

Try This may not have been as successful as *M!ssundaztood*, but it was not a failure. In fact, Pink won an award for one of its singles. In 2004, she received the Grammy for Best Female Rock Vocal Performance for "Trouble." It was her first Grammy for her own work.

To promote her third album, Pink returned to the road. Some of her 2004 Try This Tour performances were captured on video and released on DVD as *P!nk: Live in Europe*. The video went gold. The release includes 27 songs, including singles from her previous albums.

Even with less-than-stellar sales from *Try This*, Pink was still an undeniable favorite with fans near and far. She kept moving forward in her career. In the midst of writing, recording, and promoting music, she was also broadening her personal life. And soon her personal and professional lives would collide.

||||||||||

In true Pink style, the pop star used the lackluster success of *Try This* to fuel her next goals.

As Pink's professional career moved forward, so did her personal life.

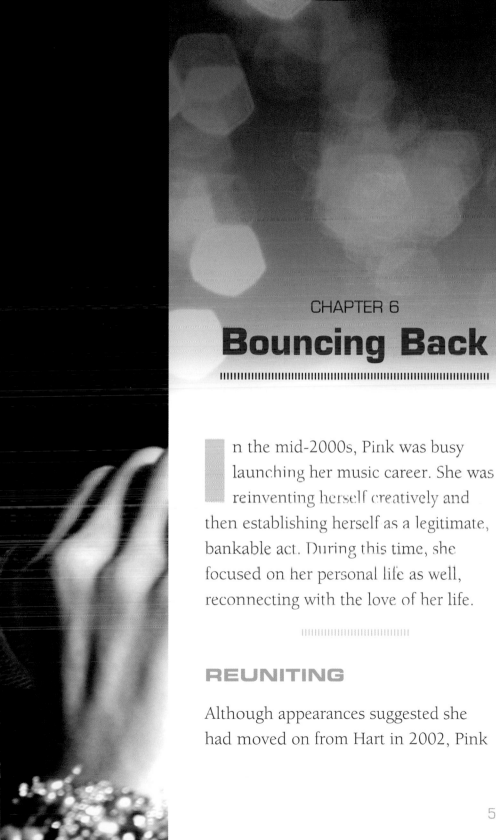

CHAPTER 6

Bouncing Back

||||||||||||||||||||||||||||||||||||||||||||||||||||||||||||||||||||||||||||||||||||||

I n the mid-2000s, Pink was busy launching her music career. She was reinventing herself creatively and then establishing herself as a legitimate, bankable act. During this time, she focused on her personal life as well, reconnecting with the love of her life.

|||||||||||||||||||||||||||||||

REUNITING

Although appearances suggested she had moved on from Hart in 2002, Pink still loved him. Hart still had feelings for her as well. They began hanging out again in 2005, and then she took a big step in June. Hart had a race in Mammoth Lakes, California. Pink attended, working as part of the pit crew. Her job was to be a pit boarder, standing on the edge of the track with a special board to write messages on. Pit boarders communicate with racers while they are racing.

Pink used the opportunity to do more than share race information. She held up a pit board for Hart to read as he made a lap. She had written a question on it: "Will you marry me?"[1] Hart saw

A LOVE OF TATTOOS

Pink and Hart have something in common: tattoos. Pink has more than 20 tattoos.[2] They come in many shapes and sizes, including dog tags on her ankle to honor her father and brother, who have both served in the military. A tattoo on one of her arms is in memory of a beloved dog that died: Sir Corkey Moore. She and Hart have matching tattoos. "Tru Luv" is tattooed on their wrists.[3]

Hart is passionate about tattoos and co-owns Hart & Huntington Tattoo Company, with locations in several cities. It turns out Pink would start over if she could with her tattoos, though. She said, "I can explain every single one of 'em and have a good laugh. But if I could start over, I'd do just one big back piece and have a clean [front]. I'm into balance."[4]

Newlyweds Pink and Hart were all smiles after tying the knot in January 2006.

the board and kept racing. To make sure he knew she was not simply playing a joke, Pink added to her message: "I'm serious!" [5] Those words got Hart's attention when he came around on the next lap. He pulled off the track and went to Pink. He accepted her proposal.

Less than one year later, the couple wed. On January 7, 2006, Pink and Hart married on a beach in Costa Rica. Hart explained, "We wanted it very fun and nontraditional. We're spiritual, but we're not religious. It was being with our closest friends and family and having a very fun and loose party."[6]

‖‖‖‖‖‖‖‖‖‖‖‖‖‖‖‖‖‖‖‖‖‖‖‖‖‖‖‖‖‖‖‖‖‖‖‖‖‖‖

I'M NOT DEAD

Just weeks after getting married, Pink was busy promoting her new album. The rocker cowrote 11 of the album's 14 songs. She was listed as sole writer of one song, a hidden track. That song, "I Have Seen the Rain," is a duet with her dad. The first single, "Stupid Girls," hit airwaves on February 7. Two months later, *I'm Not Dead*, Pink's fourth album, hit the market on April 4.

The album's first track, "Stupid Girls," highlights celebrities such as Britney Spears, Jessica Simpson, and Paris Hilton. Pink spoke about the

WINNING A MOONMAN

In 2006, Pink won Best Pop Video for "Stupid Girls" at the MTV Video Music Awards. Each year, MTV honors artists with the Moonman trophy in a variety of video categories. Pink has been honored with a Moonman three other times. In 2001, "Lady Marmalade" won for Best Video from a Film and for Video of the Year. In 2002, Pink won Best Female Video and Best Dance Video for "Get the Party Started."

song and accompanying video, explaining that she was sending a message:

> It was more of a social commentary on these girls, who think they have to be stick thin and have the latest handbag. There's nothing wrong with being sexy, but you have to be sexy for yourself, not society.[7]

"I wanted it to spark some sort of passion, whether it be anger or enlightenment, whatever. I wanted it to create discussion and debate and shed light on how ridiculous it all is. I look forward to controversy. . . . Any kind of effect is good."[8]

—PINK DISCUSSING "STUPID GIRLS"

The single was a hit with fans. It was one of several chart toppers on the album. "Who Knew" and "U + Ur Hand" each made the Top 10. These radio regulars helped the singer achieve another successful album. With sales in the hundreds of thousands and then millions, *I'm Not Dead* went gold and then platinum.

Critical reviews were good as well. In April 2006, Barry Walters of *Rolling Stone* gave the album three and a half out of five stars. He noted,

> Try This *fell flat in record stores, but with* I'm Not Dead, *Pink returns to reclaim her chart destiny. . . .* I'm Not Dead *swaggers with a cockiness that most dudes in bands can't match. Whether she sings rock, pop, R&B, or her usual combination of all three, the twenty-six-year-old Doylestown, Pennsylvania, native is belting more urgently and taking more risks than her pop-radio contemporaries.*[9]

||||||||||||||||||||||||||||||||||||||||||||||||||||||

HITTING THE ROAD

Pink toured to promote her latest album, hitting the road only three weeks after getting married.

> "My shows are incredibly physically demanding, even when it's not an arena show, it's just a club gig, because I'm insane and I like to jump around. And it's very hard to sing and dance at the same time. You either sound [bad] or you lipsynch, and I'd much rather sound [bad]."[10]
>
> —PINK DISCUSSING HER I'M NOT DEAD TOUR

With *I'm Not Dead*, Pink showed critics and fans alike she still had a fearless spirit and a will to succeed.

Touring would keep her on the road for two years. Pink spent part of that time touring with former *NSYNC singer Justin Timberlake. From January to July 2007, the two would perform in the United States and Europe. While it was great for her career, the touring once again put a strain on Pink's relationship with Hart. The newlyweds would be apart for weeks at a time.

With a new marriage plus a new album and tour, Pink was juggling a lot in 2006 and 2007. The year 2008 would reveal the truth of her relationship with Hart and would bring a major change to Pink's life.

||||||||||

In 2008, Pink's heartache would find its way into her music.

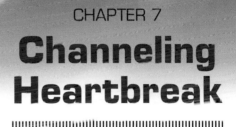

CHAPTER 7

Channeling Heartbreak

|||||||||||||||||||||||||||||||||||||||||||||||||||||||||||||||||||||||||||

With getting married and the popularity of *I'm Not Dead*, Pink experienced personal and professional success in 2006 and 2007. In early 2008, however, the dynamo suffered a heartbreaking personal loss.

|||||||||||||||||||||||||||||||||||||||

BREAKING UP

By February 2008, after two years of marriage, Pink and Hart were struggling with their relationship. With Pink on tour, the husband and wife would not see each other for weeks at a time. The time apart hurt their relationship, just as it had when they dated. So much so, they decided to split. They separated, but did not divorce. Pink put out a statement about the split: "This decision was made by best friends with a huge amount of love and respect for one another. While the marriage is over, their friendship has never been stronger."[1]

"Happiness makes me useless. Anger and sadness are inspiring. I don't have an edit button. I wish I did sometimes."[2]

—PINK DISCUSSING FUNHOUSE, 2008

The separation was a huge blow. The love of her life was gone. Never one to keep her feelings to herself, she would express them in her music.

Pink tapped into intense emotions while recording *Funhouse*.

FUNHOUSE

For *Funhouse*, her fifth album, Pink worked with a variety of songwriters, cowriting all 12 songs. Pink poured her heartbreak into her music. She cried the first two weeks of making the album as she processed what happened with Hart. Channeling her emotions would create a chart-topping album with multiple radio hits. LaFace released *Funhouse* on October 28, 2008. The album landed on *Billboard*'s album chart at Number 2.

"So What" was the album's first single. The song was meant to be a joke. Pink sings about going out, having fun, and getting into fights after the split. She even refers to Hart as a "tool."[3] LaFace wanted to release it as the album's first single. Pink agreed, but only if Hart could be in the video. She explained, "I knew that if he were in the video, it would take the sting out of it for him, and it would give me a chance to see him again."[4]

Hart agreed. After several months of separation, Hart joined Pink on the set of the "So What" video. The situation was awkward at first, but the result was an entertaining video that showcases Pink's

PINK UNDERRATED

In October 2009, James Montgomery reviewed Pink on MTV's Web site. The title of his article sums up its topic: "Pink: The World's Most Underrated Superstar." He wrote,

"If you were to make a list of the biggest pop stars, Pink probably wouldn't even crack the top five. This doesn't seem right to me, though I think I understand why it tends to happen. Unlike Britney [Spears] or [Lady] Gaga or Christina [Aguilera] or Miley [Cyrus] or Taylor [Swift], Pink is not a pure pop star. She's multifaceted, an amalgamation of many things and many eras, not easily categorized or digested."[5]

humor. She drove a riding lawnmower on a busy street, attacked a pair of newlyweds, set her hair on fire, and cut down a tree with "Alecia + Carey" carved in it.[6] More important, the video gave her and Hart, who really did love each other still, a chance to see each other.

"So What" was an undeniable hit. The post-breakup tune reached the top of the charts, becoming Pink's first Number 1 single since "Lady Marmalade." She gave a raucous performance of the song at the 2008 MTV Video Music Awards. Other tracks from the album broke the Top 20 as well, including "Please Don't Leave Me" and "Sober."

Christian Hoard reviewed the album for *Rolling Stone*. He gave *Funhouse* three stars out of five. He summed up, "*Funhouse* would be more fun if Pink went easier on the bad-love songs."[7] Other reviewers took different perspectives. Lucy Davies reviewed the album for the BBC. She noted, "Post-real life marriage split-up, she swings us round 45 minutes of joyous, out-of-control relationship breakdown, with the odd drunken diversion thrown in for good measure."[8]

Pink's performance of "So What" at the MTV Video Music Awards was complete with explosions and stunts.

Reviews aside, Pink's pain had a positive result. She transformed her feelings into another successful album. *Funhouse* reached gold and then platinum on the same day, March 3, 2009. The album sold 1 million copies in approximately five months.[9] More than four years after its release, the album was still selling, reaching double platinum status on February 4, 2013.

FUNHOUSE ON TOUR

In 2009, Pink returned to touring. The Funhouse Tour would prove to be just as successful as the album. She entertained audiences in Australia, Europe, and the United States with a carnival-themed presentation. Putting her gymnastics training to work, she took to the air, performing aerial acrobatics while singing.

Michael Menachem reviewed the tour for *Billboard*. He wrote about her concert stop in New York City's Madison Square Garden:

> *Pink offered something for all her fans. . . The Las Vegas-worthy show was presented . . . as an adult playground, complete with a rowdy dance troupe, daring acrobatics, appearing and disappearing body parts, and fierce stage presence.*[10]

A FAVORITE IN AUSTRALIA

Pink is hugely popular in Australia. She initially

Melbourne.[11] In February 2009, the singer returned

Always outspoken in her music and her passions, Pink is also an advocate for animals. The singer-songwriter has supported and promoted a variety of animal rights causes around the world. She has spoken on behalf of People for the Ethical Treatment of Animals (PETA) regarding sheep in Australia, where wool is a major industry. She is also a spokesperson for Australia's Royal Society for the Prevention of Cruelty to Animals. Pink also advocates for shelter dogs, encouraging friends to adopt them. She hosted a dog party with PETA. Pink even declined performing for the United Kingdom's Prince William's twenty-first birthday because she disagrees with his hunting practices. At Paris's famous fashion week in 2009, Pink expressed her antifur stance by lending her voice to a PETA video.

While 2008 was a difficult year for Pink, channeling her heartbreak into her new album proved to be a successful decision professionally. But on a personal level, it also gave Pink a chance to reconnect with Hart. New beginnings were around the corner.

||||||||||

The Funhouse Tour showcased Pink's showmanship as well as athleticism.

With her life back in swing, Pink had her sights set on bigger and better things in 2009 and 2010.

CHAPTER 8

A Yummy Life

||||||||||||||||||||||||||||||||||||||||||||||||||||||||||||||||||||||

After a year of heartbreak, Pink kicked off 2009 with a bang: she and Hart reunited on January 1. Pink presented Hart with a handmade scrapbook filled with mementos from their past—and a message that their future was still a possibility. With dedication, a lot of hard work, and marriage counseling, Pink and Hart reconciled, having avoided a divorce. They officially announced

With her marriage back in full swing, Pink recorded a message for the Love Is Louder campaign in 2010. Love Is Louder aims "to support anyone feeling mistreated, misunderstood, or alone."[2] In her video supporting the project, Pink said, "Love is louder than fear; love is louder than ignorance; love is louder than pain; love is louder than anything. If there's any bullies out there that really need to take their anger out on someone, come find me."[3]

their reunion in February 2010. Hart said of their relationship,

> We are both so connected and so in love that nothing's going to tear us apart. It goes beyond just the friends, the lovers, the husband and wife. I mean, we definitely are soul mates.[1]

||||||||||||||||||||||||||||||||||||||||||||||||||||||

STANDING OVATION

With her love life renewed, Pink got off to a great start professionally as well in 2010. At the end of January, she gave her unforgettable performance of "Glitter in the Air" at the Grammys. Her aerial acrobatics were a mere sampling of the Funhouse Tour performance fans worldwide had seen.

Pink's appearance at the Grammys garnered the singer a lot of attention. She appeared on *The Oprah Winfrey Show* just days after the performance. Winfrey exclaimed she had moved closer to her television during the telecast, amazed by Pink's acrobatics. Winfrey said, "That was a jaw-dropping, ceiling-hanging, almost-naked, ripped-body situation."[4]

Pink noted she was nervous when she first walked out on stage but got more comfortable once airborne. The pop star also said she thinks she sings better upside down. Pink felt proud of the performance, saying, "I didn't fall; I didn't mess up the words. That was a good night for me."[5] She admitted the best part of the night was the audience's reaction. "For me, it was when everyone stood up at the end."[6]

Winfrey asked Pink about her choice to perform that particular song. Pink explained:

It feels like after 10 years people still don't know what I do. [The song is] very spiritual and it's very sensual and it's very sophisticated and visually beautiful, so I just wanted to really show up.[7]

||||||||||||||||||||||||||||||||||||||||||||||||||||||||||||||||

Pink's best-of album showcases the songs that had made
her a star.

GREATEST HITS
. . . SO FAR!!!

Pink toured during the summer of 2010, and
then that fall, on October 5, 31-year-old Pink
announced her next album. *Greatest Hits . . . So
Far!!!* would be a collection of her top hits, such
as "Get the Party Started" and "So What," plus two
new songs. She debuted the first single, a new song
titled "Raise Your Glass," that day as well.

Initially, Pink did not want to do a greatest hits album. That type of album simply did not excite her. She thought it would be something for much later in her career. Her record company disagreed. And her label did not need Pink's approval to put out a compilation album. Pink joined in the process to gain some control over it.

The best-of album dropped on November 16. By the time the album was available, "Raise Your Glass" was racing up the charts. The upbeat song was another misfit anthem with the singer cheering, "Raise your glass if you are wrong in all the right ways."[8] By the beginning of December, the song was Number 1 on *Billboard*'s Hot 100.

Another new tune featured on the album, "Perfect," became the singer's seventh Number 1 on *Billboard*'s Pop Songs chart. That distinction tied her with Rihanna for the most Number 1 singles on that chart, surpassing pop divas Beyoncé, Mariah

THE FUNHOUSE SUMMER CARNIVAL TOUR

In June 2010, Pink hit the road again for the *Funhouse* album. The singer presented the Funhouse Summer Carnival Tour in June and July. That summer, she traveled Europe, performing 34 shows in 14 countries in 12 weeks.[9] Tor Nielson, a concert promoter in Sweden, said, "Pink is truly the next generation of stadium artistes."[10]

In the midst of a busy 2010, Pink joined an all-star cast of artists on *The Imagine Project*, an album by jazz artist Herbie Hancock. Hancock led Pink and others in a reimagining of John Lennon's classic "Imagine" from 1971. The other artists featured in the song are Seal, India.Arie, Konono No. 1, Jeff Beck, and Oumou Sangaré. For her portion of the song, Pink sang a duet with Seal. Pink also appears on another song on the album. "Don't Give Up" was originally a duet by Peter Gabriel and Kate Bush in 1986. Pink sang the new duet with singer-songwriter John Legend. In February 2011, "Imagine" earned Pink her third Grammy, this time for Best Pop Collaboration with Vocals.

Carey, and Lady Gaga. The song was also Pink's fifth Number 1 on the Adult Pop Songs chart, tying her with rock group Nickelback for most Number 1 singles in that list. The two hits gave Pink yet another distinction: *Greatest Hits . . . So Far!!!* was the only best-of album to feature more than one new Number 1 song.

||||||||||||||||||||||||||||||||||||||||||||||||||

"EATING FOR TWO"

Pink was riding high professionally. It turned out things were equally as good in her personal life. On November 17, 2010, the pop songstress appeared on *The Ellen DeGeneres Show* to promote her greatest hits release. But Pink also made a special announcement during her appearance. "I'm eating for two these days," she said, letting the world know she and Hart were expecting their first child.[11]

Pink went on to explain she was reluctant to talk about the pregnancy because she had been pregnant before and had a miscarriage. The mother-to-be also said to DeGeneres, "I'm terrified, because [the doctor] thinks [the baby is] a girl. My mom has always wished me a daughter just like me. I'm terrified. One of us will go to jail."[12]

A "PERFECT" BABY

The song "Perfect" from her best-of album was a chart-topping success. Pink wrote the song for the baby while she was pregnant. Pink explains the song's meaning in a post on her blog: "I have a life inside of me, and I want her or him to know that I will accept him or her with open and loving and welcoming arms. And though I will prepare this little munchkin for a sometimes cruel world, I will also equip this kid to see all the beauty in it as well."[13] Her sentiments are clear in the last line of the tune's refrain: "You are perfect to me."[14]

When Pink appeared on *Ellen* to announce her pregnancy, the television host surprised her with two special gifts perfect for Pink and Hart's baby. Much to Pink's delight, DeGeneres presented her with a baby onesie complete with "tattoo" sleeves and a miniature motocross bike. Even though the bike was clearly intended for a small child, Pink still predicted her husband would not be able to resist riding the bike that very day.

The TV host asked the singer about her marriage. Pink said she and her husband were on track and doing well:

> I never had anything in my life that I didn't work hard for and my relationship is that. We worked really hard and we had our little meltdowns, a couple of them, and now . . . we both needed to do that and come back together. It's just yummy.[15]

The year 2010 had been an amazing one for Pink. Soon, it would get better in ways she had only ever imagined.

||||||||||

In November 2010, Pink and Hart
were thrilled to announce they
were expecting their first child.

Life became even more amazing for Pink with the arrival of Willow Sage Hart.

CHAPTER 9

The Truth About Love

||||||||||||||||||||||||||||||||||||||||||||||||||||||||||

he year 2010 had been one of note for Pink. Professionally, her best-of album and two of its singles topped charts and set records. Personally, she and her husband had reunited and were expecting their first child. Life was undeniably good. In the summer of 2011, it got even better.

||||||||||||||||||||||||||||||||||||

Pink uses the latest technology to keep up with her fans. In addition to having a Web site on which she blogs, Pink is an avid tweeter. She is on Facebook, and she also posts videos on YouTube. She has taken part in at least one Web cast as well. Social media has allowed fans special access to Pink.

WELCOMING WILLOW

On June 2, 2011, 31-year-old Pink gave birth to a baby girl. The avid tweeter shared the news with her fans. She wrote of her new baby, Willow Sage Hart, "She's gorgeous, just like her daddy."[1]

Pink decided on her baby's name because of the plants it represents. The willow tree does not break easily. Rather than snapping, its branches bend. And sage is used for spiritual healing. She and her husband burn the herb to clear bad energy.

In the weeks following the birth, Pink remarked about the overwhelming sense of love between her, Hart, and their new addition. She said,

I knew when I met him he'd be a great father, but watching him fall in love, watching him nurture her, I've never been so in love with him in my life.

He keeps thanking me for giving her to him. It's a beautiful time.[2]

Pink took time off to be a full-time mother. After spending a year home with Willow, Pink returned to the studio to record her next album: *The Truth About Love.* She found that parenthood brought some changes in her professional life, too. With her new role as mother, she stopped drinking and staying up all night, which had been a common practice when she was recording previous albums. Instead, the rocker mom worked a set schedule.

|||||||||||||||||||||||||||||||||||||||||||||||||||||

NOT-SO-BAD GIRL |||||||||||||||||||||||||||||||||||||||||||||||||||||||||||||||||||||||||||||

As she awaited motherhood in 2011, celebrity news gave Pink a chance to reflect about the surprising path her life took. Pink often comes off as a bad girl in her look, her words, and her music. Some could easily mistake her for a troublemaker, but she is not. She highlighted that fact in a tweet on March 1, 2011. That day, Aguilera was arrested for public intoxication. Pink's tweet also referenced Spears, who often made headlines with her troubles from 2006 to 2008. Pink wrote, "Out of Myself, Britney, and Christina— didn't everyone think I was gonna be the troublemaker? LOOK MA!!! No CUFFS!!!"[3]

THE TRUTH ABOUT LOVE

On September 18, 2012, *The Truth About Love* dropped. Fans bought it eagerly. With 280,000 units sold in its first week, the new release went right to the top of the charts.[4] The album debuted at Number 1—marking the star's first chart-topping album. *The Truth About Love* went gold in October and platinum in December.

Pink cowrote 12 of the album's 13 songs. "Just Give Me a Reason" is a duet with Nate Ruess, lead singer of the group Fun. He cowrote the song as well. He said of the project,

> *Writing the song was a whole different learning experience and was really fueled by the fact that Alecia is so strong and independent and so very much herself. At the end of the day, it's so hard to argue against her because what she does [is] always so great.*[5]

The duo's collaboration was a hit. The song reached Number 1 on *Billboard's* Hot 100 chart in April 2013. That same month, "Just Give Me a Reason" set another record for Pink. She had more songs reach Number 1 on *Billboard's* Adult Pop Songs chart than any performer in the chart's

Pink made changes in order to balance motherhood with her career.

17-year history. As Pink evolved, so did her music and her audience. Growing as a person and as an artist helped expand her appeal and her popularity.

|||||||||||||||||||||||||||||||||||||||||||||||||||||||

THE TRUTH ABOUT LOVE TOUR

For Pink, an album is a three-year commitment: one year for writing and recording and two years for touring. She timed *The Truth About Love* based on Willow's age, planning when her daughter would be ready for traveling during the tour. The tour took the star—and Willow—from North America to Europe, on to Australia, and back to North America. She spoke about juggling marriage, motherhood, and career, finding it second nature: "I'm a Virgo," she said, referring to her zodiac sign. "It's a joke that we're perfectionists and planners, and it's totally true."[6]

By late May, she had set a new record in Australia, selling out 18 shows at Rod Laver Arena in Melbourne.[7] The record she broke was her own, which she set during the Funhouse Tour.

GETTING IN SHAPE

After giving birth to Willow, Pink had to get in shape before heading out on her new tour. She lost 55 pounds (25 kg) and got fit through a combination of exercise and healthy eating. She admits the process was slow, especially because she had a cesarean section to deliver Willow.

For exercise, Pink usually does a combination of activities. She will do cardio for an hour, plus strength work or yoga. For her diet, the star sometimes eats chicken and fish, but she tends to be a vegetarian. She will also eat a vegan diet, which excludes all animal products.

Pink's Truth About Love Tour wowed concertgoers across the globe.

In mid-June 2013, initial tour numbers came in. The North American leg that ran from February 13 to March 28 and included 21 shows was a huge success according to *Billboard*. Pink earned gross sales of almost $23.7 million, playing to more than 315,000 fans.[8] She topped the Hot Tours chart that week.

With a strong and healthy marriage, a wonderful baby daughter, and a record-breaking tour, Pink was on top. Her possibilities seem endless.

||||||||||

Pink's life and career have taken her far from her troubled beginnings.

CHAPTER 10

The Truth About Pink

||||||||||||||||||||||||||||||||||||||||||||||||||||||||||||||

N ow in her thirties, Pink is far from the child who grew up in a broken family or the teenager performing with a fake ID in clubs. In her second decade as a chart-topping act, Pink is a reliable, bankable artist, with every one of her solo albums reaching platinum status, some of them multiple times.

Pink is also reliably unpredictable in a sense, still shunning the usual mold for pop stars. The once dangerous and self-destructive youth is now a devoted wife and doting mother. And professionally, the star seems to continue rising as she keeps putting out hits and selling out stadiums.

NEXT MOVES

Beyond her Truth About Love Tour, Pink's future career ventures are unknown. Regarding music, Pink has expressed interest in taking her songwriting in a new direction. The pop star

PINK'S POPULARITY ||||||||||||||||||||||||||||||||||||||||||||||||||||||||||||||||||||||||||||||||||||||

With her talent, daring, and indisputable success, one might ask why the chart-topping singer is not even more popular, reaching megastar status on the level of Beyoncé. Rob Sheffield of *Rolling Stone* commented on her place in the pop spectrum: "I think people respond to her sense of independence and dedication. It inspires people. This is a prolific pop artist who is sometimes famous and successful, sometimes obscure, who nonetheless keeps making her own kind of music. Every few years, the spotlight comes back around to her—but her fans can trust that when the spotlight moves along, Pink will keep on writing Pink songs."[1]

Pink considers performing as the key to her career now and in the future.

would like to work with songwriters in Nashville, Tennessee, the home of country music. Her goal would be to dig even deeper into her inner workings with her music for creativity's sake, not only to produce music that will be popular.

When considering her future as a performer, the pop star has likened herself to Cher. The legendary singer's record-breaking career has included a Number 1 single in each of six decades. Pink once said,

If I'm Cher, say, this is the first quarter of my career. In about 30 years, I will for sure be in Vegas . . . Carey's from Vegas; I told him baby,

one day we'll be back there. I want Celine Dion's
room at Caesars Palace![2]

As Pink explores other entertainment avenues, it seems there would be a place for her on television, given the abundance of talent shows. She has been asked to be a judge on the popular singing programs *American Idol* and *X Factor*. People have also suggested she and Hart do a reality show letting viewers into their everyday life. But a television show of any kind is simply not something Pink wants to do.

"It's not that I don't want to do one. [I say no] just out of spite for everyone else doing one and it being so . . . annoying. I believe that [a reality show with her and Hart] would be very entertaining, but no thank you. I've been asked to do *American Idol* and *X Factor*. . . . It's just not for me."[3]

—PINK DISCUSSING THE POSSIBILITY OF BEING ON TELEVISION

In terms of what is next for her family, having more children seems likely. Pink sees herself with a houseful of children—and pets:

I want a basketball team. It's the best thing I've done. In 10 years, I'll have an 11-year-old and an eight-year-old and a five-year-old and a three-year-old and a six-month-old and 18 dogs, a horse and a pig.[4]

OLDER, WISER—BUT STILL PINK

Life has shaped the person Pink has become. Her experiences as a troubled youth, performer, wife, and mother have each played a part. In September 2012, as Pink was launching her Truth About Love Tour, she reflected on being a veteran in the music business:

We do . . . awesome, we play crazy places, I'm . . . headlining . . . and I'm happy. I'm never gonna be on the cover of a bunch of glossy magazines. If it was a popularity contest, I'm not gonna win, and I'm so . . . cool with that.[5]

In that same interview, she also revealed personal growth. She admitted how five years earlier, she was not as secure with her place in the so-called popularity contest of the music industry

In 2012, Pink took on another new role: model. In August of that year, she signed a contract to be a cover girl after all—with the CoverGirl cosmetics company. Esi Eggleston Bracey, the company's vice present and general manager, said of the partnership, "P!nk is a powerful and provocative role model, who has always been an advocate of individualism and making no apologies for who you are. That combination of irreverence and integrity is exactly what the CoverGirl brand loves about her and identifies with."[7]

and celebrity life. Back then, she wanted to feel accepted—to be considered popular and pretty. She felt she had to prove something. But time and experience brought a new perspective:

> *Now, life is good. Let me go on tour and those guys [other women pop stars] can do the photoshoots. I hate getting my picture taken. Now, I look at the big picture.*[6]

|||||||||||||||||||||||||||||||||||||||||||||||||||||||

TRUE TO HERSELF

When she entered the music scene, Pink was a teenager: independent, rebellious, and full of

Fans can always count on Pink to be true to herself.

in-your-face attitude. Pink has changed over the years, shaping her music to be a better reflection of herself. And along the way, she has expanded her fan base. Pink is older and wiser—but she still has that independent and rebellious attitude.

She is consistent, telling the world her thoughts and not backing down. Over time, the public has come to expect this, if not desire it. Pink is Pink, and that is why fans love her.

⦀⦀⦀⦀⦀

TIMELINE

1979

Alecia Beth Moore is born on September 8.

1987

Alecia's parents divorce, which will shape her personal and professional lives.

1995

On Thanksgiving Day, Alecia nearly overdoses on drugs. The next day, she stops taking them.

2001

Pink records "Lady Marmalade" with Christina Aguilera, Lil' Kim, and Mýa for the *Moulin Rouge!* sound track.

2001

M!ssundaztood hits shelves on November 20 and takes Pink's career in a new direction.

2003

M!ssundaztood goes five times platinum on October 22 and becomes Pink's best-selling album.

1996

L. A. Reid signs Alecia to a recording contract as part of the group Choice.

1998

Choice breaks up, and Alecia continues on with Reid as a solo artist.

2000

Pink's first solo album, *Can't Take Me Home*, is released on May 5.

2003

Try This drops on November 11.

2006

Pink marries Carey Hart on January 7.

2006

Pink's album *I'm Not Dead* becomes available on April 4.

TIMELINE

2008

In February, Pink and her husband separate.

2008

Pink's album *Funhouse* goes on sale on October 28.

2009

On January 1, Pink and Hart get back together.

2010

"So What" hits Number 1 on the Billboard Hot 100, Pink's first Number 1 since "Lady Marmalade."

2011

Pink gives birth to a daughter, Willow Sage Hart, on June 2.

2012

In August, Pink becomes a CoverGirl celebrity model.

2009

In February, Pink donates $250,000 to bushfire victims in Victoria, Australia.

2010

Pink gives a standout performance at the Grammys on January 31.

2010

Pink's album *Greatest Hits . . . So Far!!!* is released on November 16.

2012

Pink's album *The Truth About Love* drops on September 18.

2013

Pink sets a record in April, becoming the artist with the most Number 1 Adult Pop Songs in the *Billboard* chart's 17-year history.

2013

In May, Pink set a new record in Australia for sold-out shows, beating the previous record she had set.

FULL NAME

Alecia Beth Moore

DATE OF BIRTH

September 8, 1979

PLACE OF BIRTH

Doylestown, Pennsylvania

MARRIAGE

Carey Hart (January 7, 2006–)

CHILDREN

Willow Sage Hart

ALBUMS

Can't Take Me Home (2000), *M!ssundaztood* (2001), *Try This* (2003), *I'm Not Dead* (2006), *Funhouse* (2008), *Greatest Hits . . . So Far!!!* (2010), *The Truth About Love* (2012)

TOURS

Pink's Party (2002), Try This (2004), I'm Not Dead (2006–2007), Funhouse (2009), Funhouse Summer Carnival (2010), The Truth About Love (2013)

SELECTED FILM APPEARANCES

Rollerball (2002), *Charlie's Angels: Full Throttle* (2003), *Catacombs* (2007), *Get Him to the Greek* (2010), *Happy Feet Two* (2011), *Thanks for Sharing* (2013)

SELECTED AWARDS

- Won 2001 Grammy for Best Pop Collaboration with Vocals ("Lady Marmalade")
- Won 2003 Grammy for Best Female Rock Vocal Performance ("Trouble")
- Won 2010 Grammy for Best Pop Collaboration with Vocals ("Imagine")

PHILANTHROPY

For years, Pink has been a supporter of animal rights and has lent her celebrity to causes such as Australia's Royal Society for the Prevention of Cruelty to Animals, Love Is Louder, and PETA. Pink has also given generously to victims of bushfires in Australia, where she has a huge fan base.

> "Happiness makes me useless. Anger and sadness are inspiring. I don't have an edit button. I wish I did sometimes."
>
> —PINK

GLOSSARY

Billboard—A music chart system used by the music recording industry to measure record popularity or sales.

bridge—A part of a song that connects two other parts.

chart—A weekly listing of songs or albums in order of popularity or record sales.

debut—A first appearance.

drop—To become available for sale.

exorcise—To get rid of.

genre—A category of art, music, or literature characterized by a particular style, form, or content.

Grammy Award—One of several awards the National Academy of Recording Arts and Sciences presents each year to honor musical achievement.

headliner—The main performer at a concert.

hidden track—A song on an album that is intended to be undetected by casual listeners.

intoxication—The state of being drunk.

mentor—A trusted counselor or guide.

miscarriage—The loss of a baby before it is born.

punk rock—A kind of music that typically features extreme expressions of alienation and discontent.

producer—Someone who oversees or provides money for a play, television show, movie, or album.

refrain—The chorus of a song; the part of a song that is repeated.

rhythm and blues (R&B)—A kind of music that—especially in modern times—typically combines hip-hop, soul, and funk.

single—An individual song that is distributed on its own over the radio and other mediums.

studio—A room with electronic recording equipment where music, television, or film is recorded.

tempo—The speed at which a song is played. Up-tempo is fast; down-tempo is slow.

track—A portion of a recording contract containing a single song or a piece of music.

unit—One sale of a song or album, either digitally or physically.

ADDITIONAL RESOURCES

SELECTED BIBLIOGRAPHY

"Behind the Music: Pink." *VH1*. Viacom, 2013. Web. 28 July 2013.

"Pink Biography." *Biography*. A+E Television Networks, 2013. Web. 28 July 2013.

"Pink's Jaw-Dropping Grammy Performance." *Oprah*. Harpo Productions, Inc., 5 Feb. 2010. Web. 28 July 2013.

FURTHER READINGS

Kallen, Stuart A. *The History of American Pop*. Farmington Hills, MI: Lucent, 2012. Print.

Lester, Paul. *Split Personality: The Story of P!NK*. London: Music Sales Group, 2009. Print.

WEB SITES

To learn more about Pink, visit ABDO Publishing Company online at **www.abdopublishing.com**. Web sites about Pink are featured on our Book Links page. These links are routinely monitored and updated to provide the most current information available.

PLACES TO VISIT

Doylestown Business and Community Alliance

63 E. State St.
Doylestown, PA 18901
215-340-9988
http://doylestownalliance.org
This organization keeps the local traditions alive in
Pink's hometown.

Grammy Museum

800 W. Olympic Blvd., Ste. A245
Los Angeles, CA 90015
213-765-6800
http://www.grammymuseum.org
Learn about a variety of music forms, the creative process,
the history of the awards, and more through more than two
dozen exhibits.

SOURCE NOTES

CHAPTER 1. "GLITTER IN THE AIR"

1. Ben Sisario. "Big Grammy Ratings, but Less Impressive Sales." *NYTimes.com*. New York Times, 10 Feb. 2010. Web. 28 July 2013.

2. Mark Menachem. "Pink/October 5, 2009/New York (Madison Square Garden)." *Billboard*. Billboard, 7 Oct. 2009. Web. 28 July 2013.

3. "P!nk—Glitter in the Air (Grammys on CBS)." *YouTube.com*. YouTube.com, 2 Feb. 2010. Web. 28 July 2013.

4. "Pink Had Grammy Fall Fear." *Boston.com*. New York Times, 1 Feb. 2010. Web. 28 July 2013.

5. "P!nk—Glitter in the Air (Grammys on CBS)." *YouTube.com*. YouTube.com, 2 Feb. 2010. Web. 28 July 2013.

6. James Montgomery. "Pink: The World's Most Underrated Superstar." *MTV.com*. Viacom International, 7 Oct. 2009. 28 July 2013.

CHAPTER 2. PINK'S ROOTS

1. "Pink Biography." *Biography.com*. A+E Television Networks, 2013. Web. 28 July 2013.

2. "Pink Learned 'The Truth About Love.'" *USA Today*. Gannett, 18 Sept. 2012. Web. 28 July 2013.

3. Ibid.

4. "Pink Biography." *Biography.com*. A+E Television Networks, 2013. Web. 28 July 2013.

5. "Behind the Music: Pink." *VH1.com*. Viacom International, 2012. Web. 28 July 2013.

6. "Pink Biography." *Biography.com*. A+E Television Networks, 2013. Web. 28 July 2013.

7. "Behind the Music: Pink." *VH1.com*. Viacom International Inc. 2012. Web. 28 July 2013.

8. Julie Wang. "Pink Biography." *People.com*. Time Inc., 2013. Web. 28 July 2013.

9. "Pink Learned 'The Truth About Love.'" *USA Today*. Gannett, 18 Sept. 2012. Web. 28 July 2013.

CHAPTER 3. GETTING SIGNED

1. "Behind the Music: Pink." *VH1.com*. Viacom International, 2012. Web. 28 July 2013.

2. Ibid.

3. Ibid.

4. "Searchable Database." *RIAA.com*. RIAA, 2013. Web. 28 July 2013.

5. Njai Joszor. "Pink Celebrates 'No Cuffs' after Christina Aguilera Arrest, Britney Spears?" *Examiner.com*. Clarity Digital Group, 1 Mar. 2011. Web. 28 July 2013.

6. Douglas Wolk. "Pink: Can't Take Me Home." *RollingStone.com*. Rolling Stone, 27 Apr. 2000. Web. 28 July 2013.

7. Julie Wang. "Pink Biography." *People.com*. Time Inc., 2013. Web. 28 July 2013.

CHAPTER 4. EVOLVING HER SOUND

1. "Behind the Music: Pink." *VH1.com*. Viacom International, 2012. Web. 28 July 2013.

2. Julie Wang. "Pink Biography." *People.com*. Time, 2013. Web. 28 July 2013.

3. "Searchable Database." *RIAA.com*. RIAA, 2013. Web. 28 July 2013.

4. "Pink Lyrics: 'Don't Let Me Get Me.'" *AZLyrics.com*. AZLyrics.com, 2013. Web. 28 July 2013.

5. Rob Sheffield. "M!ssundaztood." *RollingStone.com*. Rolling Stone, 13 Nov. 2001. Web. 28 July 2013.

CHAPTER 5. *TRY THIS*

1. "Pink: Album Guide." *RollingStone.com*. Rolling Stone, 2013. Web. 28 July 2013.

2. Jon Wiederhorn, Iann Robinson, and Meridith Gottlieb. "Rancid Frontman Says He'd Do Anything for His Homegirl Pink; Gwen's on Deck." *MTV.com*. Viacom International, 6 Oct. 2003. Web. 28 July 2013.

3. Wes Orshoski. "Pink Colors New Album in Hues of Punk." *Boston.com*. New York Times, 8 Nov. 2003. Web. 28 July 2013.

4. Ibid.

5. Barry Walters. "Try This." *RollingStone.com*. Rolling Stone, 10 Nov. 2003. Web. 28 July 2013.

CHAPTER 6. BOUNCING BACK

1. Helena De Bertodano. "Pink Interview: 'I Don't Live in the Hollywood Bubble.'" *Telegraph*. Telegraph Media Group, 13 Dec. 2012. Web. 28 July 2013.

2. "The Ellen Degeneres Show P!nk Interview." *YouTube.com*. YouTube.com, 21 Nov. 2010. Web. 28 July 2013.

3. Andrew Macpherson. "Pink Marries Boyfriend in Costa Rica." *People.com*. Time, 8 Jan. 2006. Web. 28 July 2013.

4. Craig McLean. "Pink: 'If It Was a Popularity Contest, I'm Not Gonna Win.'" *The Independent*. Independent.co.uk, 16 Sept. 2012. Web. 18 June 2013.

5. Helena De Bertodano. "Pink Interview: 'I Don't Live in the Hollywood Bubble.'" *Telegraph*. Telegraph Media Group, 13 Dec. 2012. Web. 28 July 2013.

6. Andrew Macpherson. "Pink Marries Boyfriend in Costa Rica." *People.com*. Time, 8 Jan. 2006. Web. 28 July 2013.

7. Julie Wang. "Pink Biography." *People.com*. Time, 2013. Web. 28 July 2013.

8. "Pink—Interview—Talks About Her I'm Not Dead Tour." *YouTube*. YouTube.com, 15 Jan. 2007. Web. 27 June 2013.

9. Barry Walters. "I'm Not Dead." *RollingStone.com*. Rolling Stone, 4 Apr. 2006. Web. 28 July 2013.

10. "Pink—Interview—Talks About Her I'm Not Dead Tour." *YouTube*. YouTube.com, 15 Jan. 2007. Web. 27 June 2013.

CHAPTER 7. CHANNELING HEARTBREAK

1. "Pink and Carey Hart Divorcing." *HuffingtonPost.com*. TheHuffingtonPost.com, 19 Feb. 2008. Web. 28 July 2013.

2. Jessica Herndon. "Smash Single." *People*. Time, 3 Nov. 2008. 19 June 2013.

3. "So What Lyrics." *MetroLyrics.com*. MetroLyrics.com, 2013. Web. 28 July 2013.

4. "Behind the Music: Pink." *VH1.com*. Viacom International Inc. 2012. Web. 28 July 2013.

5. James Montgomery. "Pink: The World's Most Underrated Superstar." *MTV.com*. Viacom International, 7 Oct. 2009. Web. 28 July 2013.

6. "P!nk—So What." *YouTube.com*. YouTube.com, 24 Oct. 2009. Web. 28 July 2013.

7. Christian Hart. "Pink: Funhouse." *Rolling Stone*. Rolling Stone, 30 Oct. 2008. Web. 19 June 2013.

8. Lucy Davies. "Don't Underestimate Pink!" *BBC*. BBC, 28 Oct. 2013. Web. 19 June 2013.

9. "Searchable Database." *RIAA.com*. RIAA, 2013. Web. 28 July 2013.

10. Mark Menachem. "Pink/October 5, 2009/New York (Madison Square Garden)." *Billboard*. Billboard, 7 Oct. 2009. Web. 28 July 2013.

11. Jonathan Moran. "Pink Wraps Up Record-Breaking Australian Tour." *News.com.au*. News Limited, 30 Aug. 2009. Web. 28 July 2013.

12. "Pink Donates $250K to Bushfire Appeal." *ABC News* (Australian Broadcasting Corporation). ABC, 16 Feb. 2009. Web. 28 July 2013.

13. "Bushfire History—Major Bushfires in Victoria." *Department of Environment and Primary Industries*. The State of Victoria, 20 Apr. 2013. Web. 28 July 2013.

CHAPTER 8. A YUMMY LIFE

1. "Behind the Music: Pink." *VH1.com*. Viacom International Inc. 2012. Web. 28 July 2013.

2. James Montgomery. "Pink: The World's Most Underrated Superstar." *MTV.com*. Viacom International Inc., 7 Oct. 2009. Web. 28 July 2013.

3. "The Movement." *LoveIsLouder.com*. Love Is Louder, n.d. Web. 28 July 2013.

4. Pink's Jaw-Dropping Grammy Performance." *Oprah.com*. Harpo Productions, Inc., 5 Feb. 2010. Web. 19 June 2013.

5. Ibid.

6. Ibid.

7. Ibid.

8. "Behind the Music: Pink." *VH1.com*. Viacom International, 2012. Web. 28 July 2013.

9. Andre Paine. "Pink Moves 3 Million Tickets with Funhouse." *Billboard*. Billboard, 9 Aug. 2010. Web. 28 July 2013.

10. Ibid.

11. "The Ellen Degeneres Show P!nk Interview." *YouTube.com*. YouTube.com, 11 Nov. 2010. Web. 28 July 2013.

12. "The Ellen Degeneres Show P!nk Interview." *YouTube.com*. YouTube.com, 11 Nov. 2010. Web. 28 July 2013.

13. US Weekly. "Pink Gives Birth to Baby Girl." *RollingStone.com*. Rolling Stone, 3 June 2011. Web. 28 July 2013.

14. Pink. "Perfect Lyrics." *MetroLyrics.com*. MetroLyrics.com, 2013. Web. 27 June 2013.

15. "The Ellen Degeneres Show P!nk Interview." *YouTube.com*. YouTube.com, 11 Nov. 2010. Web. 28 July 2013.

CHAPTER 9. *THE TRUTH ABOUT LOVE*

1. US Weekly. "Pink Gives Birth to Baby Girl." *RollingStone.com*. Rolling Stone, 3 June 2011. Web. 28 July 2013.

2. Anya Leon and Marisa Laudadio. "Pink Was 'Looking Forward' to a Natural Birth." *People.com*. Time Inc., 5 July 2011. Web. 28 July 2013.

3. "Out of Myself, Britney, and Christina—didn't everyone think I was gonna be the troublemaker? LOOK MA!!! No CUFFS!!!" *Twitter.com*. Twitter, 1 Mar. 2011. Web. 28 July 2013.

4. Grady Smith. "Album Sales: Pink Scores Her First No. 1, Kanye Rides in Second—but Carly Rae Jepsen's 'Kiss' Is a Miss." *EW.com*. Entertainment Weekly Inc., 26 Sept. 2012. Web. 28 July 2013.

5. Chris Kim and Eric Ditzian. "Ruess Catches UP with MTV News at Sundance to Talk about the 'Unbelievable' Video for 'Just Give Me a Reason.'" *MTV.com*. Viacom International, 22 Jan. 2013. Web. 28 July 2013.

6. Dave Karger. "Fifty Shades of Pink." *EW.com*. Entertainment Weekly, Inc., 31 Aug. 2012. Web. 28 July 2013.

7. Lars Brandle. "Pink's Australian Tour Adds Record 18th Show at Rod Laver Arena." *Billboard*. Billboard, 27 May 2013. Web. 28 July 2013.

8. Bob Allen. "P!nk Takes No. 1 Spot on Hot Tours Chart, Grosses $25.6 Million." *Billboard*. Billboard, 14 June 2013. Web. 28 July 2013.

CHAPTER 10. THE TRUTH ABOUT PINK

1. Ann Powers. "The Many Shades of Pink—So Far." *Los Angeles Times*. Los Angeles Times, 21 Dec. 2010. Web. 28 July 2013.

2. Ibid.

3. Dave Karger. "Fifty Shades of Pink." *EW.com*. Entertainment Weekly, Inc., 31 Aug. 2012. Web. 28 July 2013.

4. Helena De Bertodano. "Pink Interview: 'I Don't Live in the Hollywood Bubble.'" *Telegraph*. Telegraph Media Group, 13 Dec. 2012. Web. 28 July 2013.

5. Craig McLean. "Pink: 'If It Was a Popularity Contest, I'm Not Gonna Win.'" *The Independent*. Independent.co.uk, 16 Sept. 2012. Web. 18 June 2013.

6. Ibid.

7. Carolyn Menyes. "P!nk Is the Newest CoverGirl: 'Beauty with an Edge.'" *Billboard*. Billboard, 6 Aug. 2012. Web. 28 July 2013.

INDEX

ABOUT THE AUTHOR

Rebecca Rowell has authored books for young readers on a variety of topics, including education advocate Malala Yousafzai, pioneer aviator Charles Lindbergh, the country of Switzerland, weather and climate, and wildfires. One of her favorite parts of writing is doing research and learning about all kinds of subjects. She has a master's degree in publishing and writing from Emerson College and lives in Minneapolis, Minnesota. She is a fan of Pink as a performer and as a person.